CHRISTMAS FAVORITES

CONTENTS

Harmonica by Steve Cohen

ISBN 978-1-4234-9464-5

Visit Hal Leonard Online at
www.halleonard.com

HAL•LEONARD®
CORPORATION
7777 W. BLUEMOUND RD. P.O. BOX 13819
MILWAUKEE, WISCONSIN 53213

Blue Christmas

Words and Music by Billy Hayes and Jay Johnson

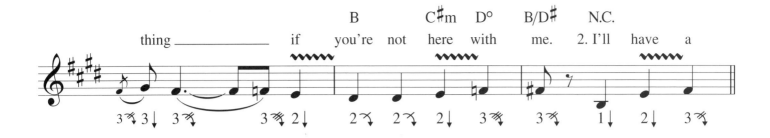

Verse

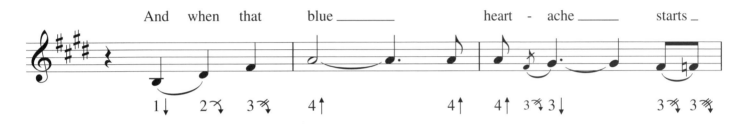

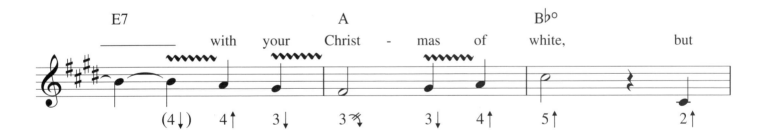

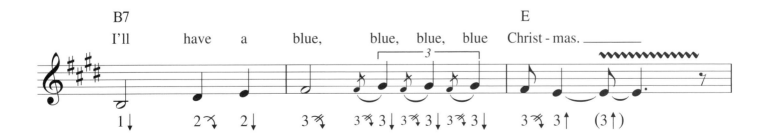

Verse

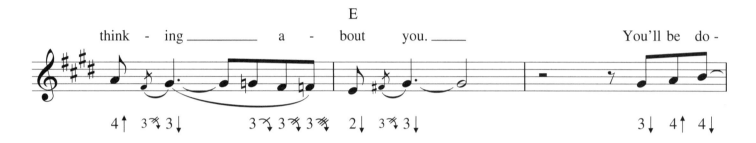

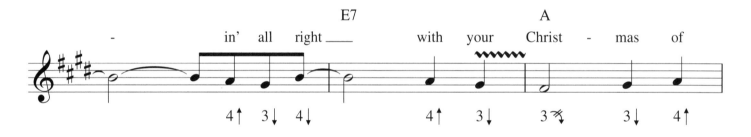

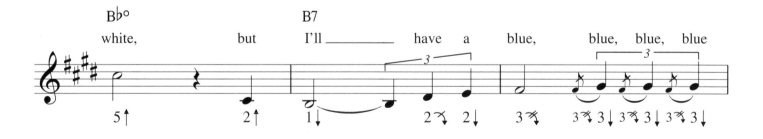

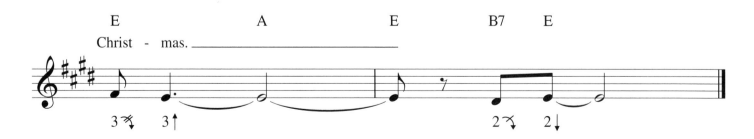

4

Frosty the Snow Man

Words and Music by Steve Nelson and Jack Rollins

HARMONICA

Harp Key: E♭ Diatonic

*Play cue note 2nd time

Bridge

Verse

6

Jingle-Bell Rock

Words and Music by Joe Beal and Jim Boothe

HARMONICA

Harp Key: C Diatonic

*Throat vibrato throughout

9

Here Comes Santa Claus
(Right Down Santa Claus Lane)

Words and Music by Gene Autry and Oakley Haldeman

HARMONICA

Harp Key: D Diatonic

*Throat vibrato throughout

11

Nuttin' for Christmas

Words and Music by Roy Bennett and Sid Tepper

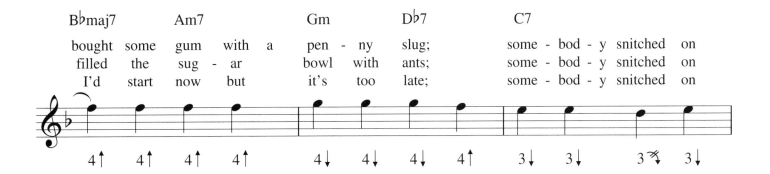

Chorus

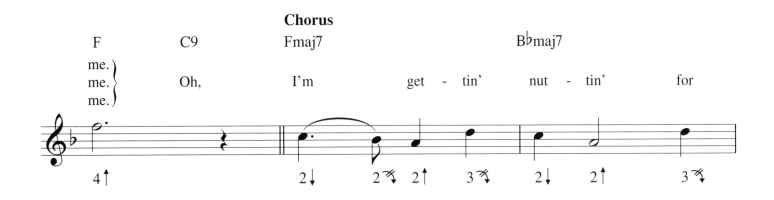

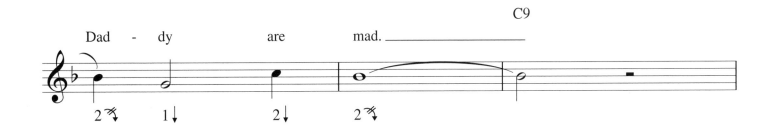

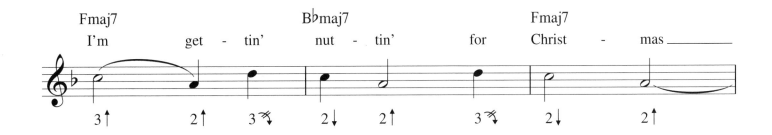

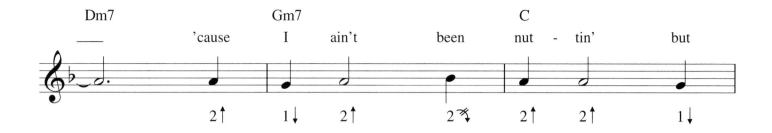

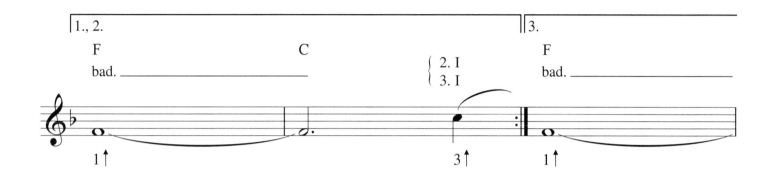

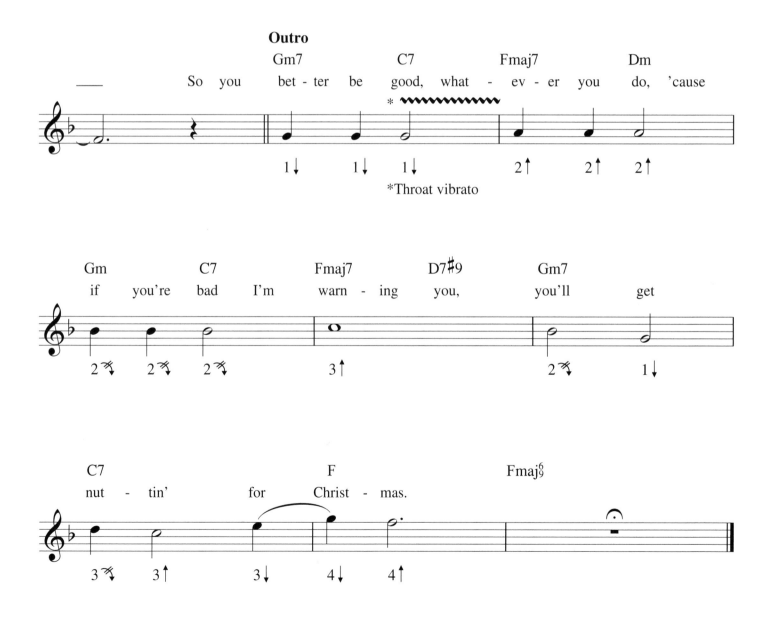

Rudolph the Red-Nosed Reindeer

Music and Lyrics by Johnny Marks

*Throat vibrato throughout

Silver Bells

from the Paramount Picture THE LEMON DROP KID
Words and Music by Jay Livingston and Ray Evans

HARMONICA

Harp Key: C Diatonic

Chorus

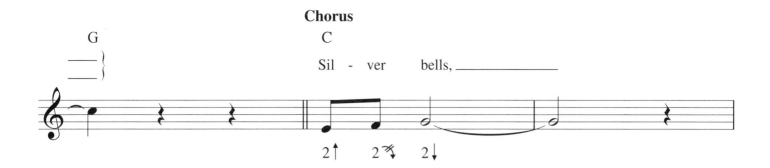

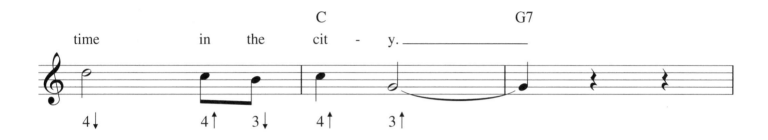

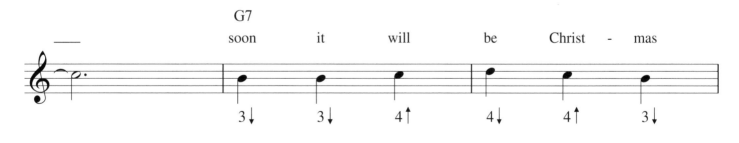

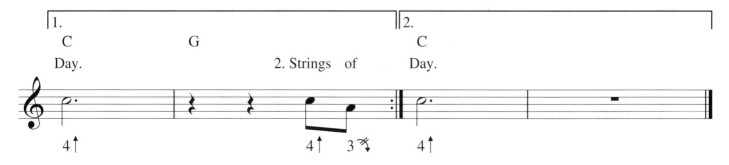

Santa Claus Is Comin' to Town

Words by Haven Gillespie
Music by J. Fred Coots

HARMONICA

Harp Key: E♭ Diatonic